TEEN WITCH

Astrid Ebonywood

CONTENTS PAGE

I. Introduction

Welcome, young witches!

If you're reading this, you're probably interested in learning more about the practice of witchcraft. Whether you're a beginner or have some experience, you've come to the right place. This book is designed to be a comprehensive guide, introducing you to the basics of witchcraft and helping you to develop your skills and knowledge.

You may feel overwhelmed by the vast amount of information and resources available. But don't worry! This book is here to help guide you on your journey, and to provide you with a solid foundation in the practice of witchcraft.

In these pages, you'll learn about the history and evolution of the craft, the basics of energy and spell casting, the significance of the elements, lunar, and planetary cycles, and much more. You'll also learn about the importance of protection, both for yourself and for your environment, as well as tips for maintaining a positive energy and avoiding negativity.

So, let's get started! Whether you're drawn to witchcraft because of a lifelong fascination with all things magical, or simply looking to connect with a sense of the spiritual, this book is the perfect introduction. By the time you reach the end, you'll have a strong understanding of the basics of witchcraft and will be well on your way to developing your own unique practice.

Good luck on your journey, young witches, and may the magic be with you!

Brightest Blessings

Astrid xx

A. Welcome Witches

The purpose of this book "Teen Witch" is to serve as a guide for all of you young, and beginner witches, (also known in some circles as baby witches) as you embark on your pathway in the practice of witchcraft.

The focus of the book is to introduce the basics of witchcraft in a way that is approachable, relatable, easy to understand and empowering to you.

This includes a deep dive into the core principles of witchcraft, including energy work, spell casting, connecting with spirit guides and deities, and incorporating nature and herbalism into your practice.

The book also covers important topics such as protection and safety, as well as tips for tracking lunar and planetary cycles and finding your personal style within the practice. With a focus on the unique challenges and experiences that come with being a young witch, and from my own personal experiences, this book is the perfect start for anyone who are looking to explore and deepen their connection to the craft.

B. The History and Evolution of Witchcraft

Witchcraft, also known as Wicca or paganism, is a spiritual practice that has been around for thousands of years, with roots tracing back to ancient civilizations such as the Celts, Greeks, and Egyptians. Over time, the practice of witchcraft evolved and was influenced by various cultures and beliefs, leading to the diverse array of traditions and practices within modern-day witchcraft.

In the Middle Ages, the craft was widely feared and persecuted, leading to the infamous witch hunts and trials. However, in the early 20th century, a revival of interest in paganism and witchcraft occurred, leading to the birth of modern Wicca and the Neo-Pagan movement. Today, witchcraft is a growing and diverse community, encompassing a wide range of beliefs across multiple countries.

Despite its long history and evolution, the core principles of witchcraft remain the same: a deep connection to nature, a focus on personal growth and self-discovery, and the belief in the power of intention and manifestation. Through the centuries, witchcraft has adapted and evolved, but its essence remains the same, offering a path of connection, empowerment, and growth for those who practice it.

C. The Basics

Witchcraft is a spiritual embodiment involving harnessing and manipulating energy bringing about desired outcomes or changes in the world. It is about connecting with the natural world and the energies that flow through it to bring about positive change in one's life and the world around them.

There are many different forms of witchcraft, including Wicca, traditional witchcraft, eclectic witchcraft, and more. Each form has its own unique set of beliefs, and practices, but they all share the core principles of energy work, spell casting, and connecting with the natural world.

The basics involve learning to work with energy and the elements, honing your practices, and connecting with spirit guides and deities This may involve learning to meditate and focus your intentions, working with tools such as candles, crystals, and herbs, and performing incantations to bring about change.

It's important to remember that witchcraft is a personal and unique practice, and what works for one person may not work for another. As a beginner witch, it's important to explore different forms of witchcraft, try new techniques, and find what resonates with you and your personal beliefs and values.

A. Energy and Witchcraft

Energy is a central concept in witchcraft and is the foundation of many of the practices and techniques found within. For witches, energy it is believed to be a force that can be harnessed, directed, and manipulated to bring about your intention.

Everything in the universe has energy, including people, animals, plants, and inanimate objects. This energy can be positive, negative, or neutral, and it can be influenced and changed by intention, emotion, and thought.

In the craft, energy work involves learning to sense and use the energy that surrounds you. This can involve techniques such as visualisation, meditation, and affirmations to focus your intentions and harness your own power. It can also involve working with the energy of the elements, fire, water, earth, air, and spirit, as well as the that of the natural world, the moon, sun, and the seasons.

By working with energy, witches are able to bring about change in the world around them, whether it be for personal growth, healing, or their desires. Energy work is a key aspect, and it's an essential tool for beginners to learn and understand as they embark on their journey in the craft.

B. The Elements

The elements are a fundamental aspect of witchcraft and play a central role in many practices and rituals within the craft. The elements are Earth, Air, Fire, Water, and Spirit, and each one is associated with different qualities, energies, and correspondences.

❖ Earth is associated with stability, growth, and material abundance. It represents the physical world and the abundance of life that can be found in the natural world.
❖ Air is associated with communication, intellectual pursuits, and inspiration. It represents the mind and the power of thought and ideas.
❖ Fire is associated with passion, transformation, and purification. It represents the spark of life, the fire within, and the power to change and purify.
❖ Water is associated with emotion, intuition, and healing. It represents the flow of life, the depth of feeling, and the power to heal and cleanse.
❖ Spirit is the final element, and it represents the essence of life, the connection to the divine, and the power of manifestation.

In witchcraft, the elements play an important role in energy work and spell casting, as they can be used to harness and direct energy towards specific goals and intentions. For example, using the energy of fire in a spell may amplify its power and bring about transformation, while using the energy of water may bring about emotional healing and balance.

By learning to work with the elements and harnessing their energies, witches are able to bring about great change in the world around them. Understanding the importance of elements and their role in witchcraft is a key trait of the craft for beginner witches to master.

C. Techniques for Harnessing Energy

There are many techniques that witches can use to connect with and harness energy, both within themselves and in the world around them. Some common techniques include:

Meditation: Meditation is a powerful tool for connecting with and harnessing energy. By focusing your mind and quieting your thoughts, you can become more in tune with yourself and the energies around you. This can help you to direct and manipulate it towards your desired outcomes.

Visualisation: Visualisation involves using your imagination to create a mental image of what you want to happen. By visualising the desired outcome in your mind, you can focus your energy and intention towards making it a reality.

Affirmations: Affirmations are positive statements that you repeat to yourself to focus your mind and on a specific goal. By repeating affirmations, you can rewire your thinking and tap into the power of your subconscious mind to bring about change.

Working with tools: Tools such as candles, crystals, and herbs can be used to focus energy and intention towards a specific goal. For example, lighting a candle during a spell can help to amplify the this and focus it towards what you are aiming for.

Connecting with the natural world: Connecting with the natural world, such as through gardening, hiking, or simply spending time in outdoors, can help you to tap into the energy of the earth and the elements, and enhance your connection with it for use in your craft.

These are just a few of the many techniques that witches can use to enhance their craft through energy. By exploring different avenues and finding what works best for you, you can become more proficient in working with energy and utilising its power towards your truth.

D. Elemental Rituals and Spells

Rituals and spells are two of the most common practices in witchcraft that involve working with the elements. By using rituals and spells, witches can use the energies of the elements and direct them towards their intensions.

For example, a spell to bring about financial abundance may involve using the energies of earth and fire to manifest material wealth and abundance in your life. A ritual to promote emotional healing may involve using the energies of water and spirit to soothe and heal emotional wounds.

When exploring the elements through rituals and spells, it's important to consider the correspondences of each element and how they can be used to bring about specific outcomes. For example, earth is associated with stability and growth, so a ritual or spell that involves earth may focus on bringing about stability and growth in your life. The previous section entitled 'The Elements' provides more detailed information on this.

It's also important however, to consider the timing of your rituals and spells, as the energies of the elements can be influenced by the phases of the moon and the cycles of the seasons. For example, performing a spell for new beginnings during the waxing moon is a common practice, as the growing energy of the moon can amplify the power of the spell. There will be more on Moon Phases later in the book.

By exploring the elements through rituals and spells, witches can tap into power in its purest form and have a great influence on their practice by doing so. Whether you are a beginner or an experienced practitioner, incorporating the elements into your work can bring deeper meaning to your intent.

A. The Power of Intention

The power of intention and visualisation is a important part of spell casting in witchcraft. In spell casting, you use your intention and visualisation to focus your energy and imagination towards a specific want or need. The goal of a spell is to bring about change, and the power of intention and visualisation helps to make this change a reality.

Intention is the driving force behind a spell. It is the energy that you put into the spell and the purpose that you have in mind. When setting your intention, it is important to be clear, concise, and focused on what you want to achieve. A strong intention can make a spell more powerful and therefore more effective.

Visualisation is the act of creating a mental image of what you want to happen. When visualising, you imagine the outcome of the spell as if it has already happened. This helps to channel your focus on the end result and makes it more likely to manifest.

Together, intention and visualisation are a powerful combination in spell casting. By setting a clear intention and visualising and your goal, you can focus core energy and bring about change. The more vivid and detailed your visualisation, the more potent your spell will be.

It's important to keep in mind that spell casting is not a guarantee that a desired outcome will occur. Casting is about putting energy and intention out into the world, but it cannot control external factors and events that may influence the change. It is also important to remember that spells can take time to manifest, and the results may not always be exactly what you expect. The power of intention and visualisation in spell work lies in the ability to focus on your wish and increase the chances of it coming to fruition.

B. Tools and Materials

Common tools and materials used in spells can include candles, herbs, crystals, oils, and symbols. Each tool and material have their own unique correspondences and can be used to enhance and focus the energy of a spell.

Candles, for example, are often used in casting to represent the elements of fire and light. Different colours of candles correspond to different things and can be used in specific spells for different purposes. For example, a green candle may be used for work related to abundance and prosperity, while a blue candle may be used for spells related to peace and tranquillity.

Herbs are also commonly used in spellcasting and are associated with specific intentions. For example, lavender is often used in spells related to peace and calming, while rosemary is used in work related to protection and purification. Herbs can be used in their natural form, or they can be incorporated into teas, baths, oils, or other spell components.

Crystals are often used in spell casting to amplify and focus the energy of the spell. Different crystals have different energies and meanings and can be used to enhance your desires. For example, amethyst is often used for spells related to spiritual growth and healing, while citrine is used is related to abundance and prosperity.

Oils are also commonly used in spells and can be used to anoint candles, crystals, or other components. Oils can also be used as a personal fragrance to enhance your own energy and to bring the desired outcome to mind.

Symbols, such as runes, tarot cards, and sigils, can also be used in spellcasting to represent the energy and intention of a spell. Symbols can be used to enhance visualization and focus the energy of the spell and can be incorporated into rituals and spells in a variety of ways.

Using tools and materials in your spells is a personal and intuitive practice. What works best for one you may not work as well for others. It is important to experiment with different tools and materials to find what resonates with you and enhances your practice.

C. Spell Casting

Here is a step-by-step guide to creating and performing spells:

1. Set your intention: Before you begin creating a spell, take some time to reflect on what you want to achieve. What is your goal or outcome? What change do you want to bring about? Be clear and concise in your intention, and make sure that it aligns with your values and beliefs.
2. Choose your tools and materials: Based on your intention, choose the tools and materials that you want to use in your spell. This may include candles, herbs, crystals, oils, or symbols, among other things. Make sure that you have all of the materials that you need before you begin your spell.
3. Create a ritual space: Find a quiet and peaceful place where you can focus and connect with your energy. Cleanse and purify the space to remove any negative energy and set up any tools or materials that you will be using in your spell.

4. Cast a circle: Casting a circle is a symbolic act that creates a protective space for your spell. You can cast a circle using your wand, hand, or any other tool that resonates with you. Imagine a circle of light and energy surrounding you and your ritual space.
5. Connect with the elements: Call upon the elements of air, fire, water, earth, and spirit to witness and support your spell. You can do this by lighting candles, burning incense, or using other symbols that represent the elements.
6. Perform the spell: This is the main event! Use your intention and visualisation to focus your energy and imagination towards your goal. Light candles, burn herbs, or use other tools and materials as you see fit. Repeat any incantations or affirmations that you have prepared and imagine the desired outcome as if it has already happened.
7. Close the circle: When your spell is complete, close the circle by thanking the elements for their support and protection. Extinguish any candles or incense and put away any tools and materials that you used.
8. Trust and release: Trust that your spell will manifest in its own time and in its own way. Release any attachment to the outcome and know that the universe is working in your favour.

Remember that spell casting is an individual and intuitive practice. There is no one right way to perform a spell, and what works for you the first time may not work your next. Experiment with different tools, materials, and techniques to find what works methods you prefer.

D. Safety Guidelines

Here are some safety tips and guidelines for spell casting:

- ❖ Know yourself: Be honest with yourself about your motivations, goals, and intentions. Make sure that your spells align with your values and beliefs and avoid casting spells for harm or manipulation.
- ❖ Respect the law of three: This is the idea that any energy you put out into the world will be returned to you threefold. Make sure that your spells are positive and in line with your highest good, as negative energy will come back to you with increased intensity.
- ❖ Use caution with candles and fire: Always supervise candles while they are burning, and make sure that they are placed on a heat-resistant surface. Avoid using candles near flammable objects, and never leave them unattended.
- ❖ Work within your limits: Spellcasting can be powerful, but it is important to work within your limits and abilities. If you are not experienced with a certain tool or technique, do your research, and seek guidance before attempting it.

❖ Be mindful of the environment: Spellcasting should be done in a safe and responsible manner that respects the environment. Avoid using materials or techniques that could harm the earth, such as single-use plastics or toxic chemicals.

❖ Seek guidance from experienced practitioners: If you are new to spellcasting, consider seeking guidance from experienced elder witches. They can help you understand the basics and offer advice on how to perform spells safely and effectively.

❖ Trust your intuition: Spellcasting is an intuitive practice, and you should always trust your gut instincts. If something doesn't feel right, don't do it. Pay attention to your body and your emotions, and adjust your spells as needed to align with your highest good.

Remember that spellcasting is an empowering practice, but it is important to take precautions and be responsible in your approach. Always prioritise your safety and well-being and seek guidance when needed.

A. Moon Phases

The phases of the moon play an important role in witchcraft, as they can influence the energy and power of spells and rituals. Here is a brief overview of the moon phases and their significance:

New Moon: The new moon is a time of new beginnings and fresh starts. It is a time to set intentions, make plans, and start new projects. This is a powerful time for spell casting, as the energy is focused on growth and manifestation.

Waxing Crescent: During the waxing crescent phase, the moon is growing and becoming more visible each night. This is a good time to focus on growth, manifestation, and attracting positive energy.

First Quarter: The first quarter is a time of balance and stability. It is a good time to focus on self-improvement and making progress towards your goals.

Waxing Gibbous: The waxing gibbous phase is a time of increasing energy and power. This is also another good time for spell casting.

Full Moon: The full moon is a time of peak energy and power. This is a time for releasing old habits, letting go of negative energy, and focusing on manifestation and growth.

Waning Gibbous: The waning gibbous phase is a time of decreasing energy and power. This is a good time to focus on protection, banishing negative energy, and releasing what no longer serves you.

Last Quarter: The last quarter is a time of reflection and renewal. It is a good time to focus on self-improvement and making changes in your life.

Waning Crescent: The waning crescent phase is a time of release and letting go. This is a good time to focus on banishing negative energy, releasing old habits, and letting go of what no longer serves your truth.

Understanding the phases of the moon can help you work with the natural energy and power of the universe. You can use this knowledge to guide your casting and rituals, and align with the energy of the moon to enhance their power and effectiveness.

B. Planetary Energies

  The planets have their own unique energies and influences, which can be harnessed in spell casting to enhance the power and efficiency of rituals. Here is a brief overview of the main planetary energies and their influences:

  Sun: The sun represents life, vitality, and creativity. It is associated with self-expression, personal power, and confidence. Working with the energy of the sun can help boost your self-esteem and bring more light and positivity into your life.

  Moon: The moon represents emotions, intuition, and the subconscious mind. It is associated with change, fertility, and the cyclical nature of life. Working with the energy of the moon can help you tap into your intuition, increase your emotional awareness, and enhance your connection to the natural world.

  Mercury: Mercury represents communication, intelligence, and travel. It is associated with learning, writing, and speaking. Working with the energy of Mercury can help improve your communication skills, enhance your ability to learn and process information, and bring more flexibility and adaptability into your life.

Venus: Venus represents love, beauty, and relationships. It is associated with creativity, pleasure, and harmony. Working with the energy of Venus can help improve your relationships, increase your sense of self-worth, and bring more beauty and joy into your life.

Mars: Mars represents action, assertiveness, and courage. It is associated with physical energy, strength, and determination. Working with the energy of Mars can help increase your confidence, improve your physical vitality, and bring more assertiveness and determination into your life.

Jupiter: Jupiter represents growth, expansion, and abundance. It is associated with wisdom, generosity, and good fortune. Working with the energy of Jupiter can help increase your abundance, bring more opportunity and growth into your life, and enhance your sense of inner wisdom.

Saturn: Saturn represents discipline, structure, and responsibility. It is associated with stability, grounding, and maturity. Working with the energy of Saturn can help increase your sense of responsibility, bring more stability and grounding into your life, and enhance your ability to achieve your goals.

Uranus: Uranus represents change, rebellion, and innovation. It is associated with unpredictability, creativity, and individuality. Working with the energy of Uranus can help bring more excitement, change, and innovation into your life, and enhance your ability to think outside the box.

Neptune: Neptune represents spirituality, intuition, and creativity. It is associated with dreams, the subconscious, and the divine. Working with the energy of Neptune can help increase your spiritual awareness, tap into your intuition, and enhance your ability to access your creative potential.

Pluto: Pluto represents transformation, power, and rebirth. It is associated with death, renewal, and the subconscious. Working with the energy of Pluto can help bring more transformation, renewal, and power into your life, and enhance your ability to tap into your subconscious mind.

By understanding the energies of the planets, you can work with their power in your spells and rituals to upgrade them by bringing more balance and harmony into your life.

C. Using the Cycles

Incorporating lunar and planetary cycles into spellcasting can help increase the charge of your spells and rituals. Here are a few ways to do so:

❖ Lunar phases: The phases of the moon have a powerful impact on spellcasting. Full moons are associated with release and manifestation, while new moons are associated with new beginnings and planting seeds. By performing spells during the appropriate lunar phase, you can harness the moon's energy to increase the potency of your magic.
❖ Planetary hours: Planetary hours are periods of time that correspond to each planet in astrology. They can be used to increase the power of spells and rituals related to specific planetary energies. For example, if you want to perform a spell related to communication and learning, you might choose to perform it during the hour of Mercury.
❖ Planetary transits: Planetary transits are when a planet moves through different signs of the zodiac. Different signs of the zodiac are associated with different energies, and by performing spells during specific planetary

transits, you can harness the energy of the planet and the sign to increase the power of your magic.

By incorporating lunar and planetary cycles into your practice, this gives you the upmost opportunity to add favour to your craft. Giving your practices the best possible chance of aligning with your wishes.

D. Tracking the Cycles

Here are some tips for tracking and utilizing lunar and planetary cycles for maximum effectiveness in spellcasting:

❖ Keep a calendar that tracks the phases of the moon and the planetary transits. You can use this calendar to plan your spells and rituals in advance and take advantage of the most favourable times for spellcasting.

❖ There are many astrological software programs and apps available that can help you track lunar and planetary cycles. These programs often include information on planetary transits, planetary hours, and other astrological data that can be useful in spellcasting.

❖ Trust your intuition when it comes to using lunar and planetary cycles in spellcasting. If you feel drawn to perform a spell during a particular phase of the moon or during a specific planetary transit, go with your gut and trust that it's the right choice for you.

❖ Don't be afraid to experiment and try new things when it comes to utilising lunar and planetary cycles. Keep records of your work and take note of what works best for you. This will help you refine your craft over time and become more effective in your spellcasting.

A. Spirit Guides and Deities

Spirit guides and deities play an important role in the practice of witchcraft. Spirit guides are non-physical entities that assist individuals in their spiritual journey, while deities are entities that represent different aspects of nature and the universe. Both can provide guidance in the practice of witchcraft, offering insight, wisdom, and protection to those who seek their assistance.

When working with them, it's important to be open to receiving messages and guidance. This may come in the form of dreams, intuition, or physical signs and symbols. Some tips for working with spirit guides and deities include setting aside dedicated time for meditation and ritual, and creating an altar to honour and connect with these entities.

It's important to approach spirit guides and deities with respect and to be mindful of ethical considerations when working with them in witchcraft. This includes being aware of cultural appropriation, avoiding using them in ways that could be harmful, and always seeking consent from these them before working. It's important to remember that these entities are not here to serve us, but rather to offer support on our spiritual journey.

B. Connecting and Communicating

There are several methods for connecting with spirit guides and deities, including meditation, ritual, and divination.

Meditation is a powerful tool for quieting the mind and opening to receive messages from the spirit world. During meditation, you can call upon your spirit guide or deity and ask for their presence and guidance.

Ritual is another effective way to connect with them. A ritual can be as simple as lighting a candle or incense and calling upon your spirit guide or deity. You can also create a more elaborate ritual, such as creating an altar and placing offerings to the entity.

Divination, such as tarot or pendulum readings, can also be used to connect with spirit guides and deities. During a divination session, you can ask specific questions and receive messages and guidance from your guide.

It is important to build a strong bond with your spirit guides and deities. This can be accomplished through regular communication, offerings, and acts of gratitude.

You can also establish specific times for communication, such as during meditation or ritual or a specific time relating to them specifically.

When working with spirit guides and deities, it is important to maintain a positive and respectful relationship. This includes honouring and showing thanks for their assistance, as well as avoiding manipulation or exploitation. Additionally, as a reminder, it is important to understand and respect the cultural and religious beliefs associated with specific deities.

C. The Common Spirit Guides and Deities

One of the most common spirit guides that a beginner witch may encounter is the animal spirit guide. These can be seen as messengers from the spirit world, bringing information and guidance. Animal spirit guides can also be invoked through meditation, visualisation, or by incorporating their symbolism into specific spells and rituals.

Nature spirits, such as fairies, elves, and gnomes, are also commonly associated with witchcraft. They are believed to reside in the natural world and can be invoked for their specific energies, such as the energy of growth and abundance.

Ancestors and angels are also commonly called upon as spirit guides. Ancestors can provide support from a personal and familial level, while angels are seen as celestial beings who offer protection from a higher perspective.

In the craft, there are many different spirit guides and deities that you may choose to work with. Some of the most common include:

❖ The Triple Goddess - representing the three phases of the moon (waxing, full, and waning) and embodies the feminine energy of the universe.

❖ The Horned God - represents the male energy of the universe and is associated with nature and the hunt.

❖ The Elementals - are spirits that are associated with the four elements of earth, air, fire, and water. They are seen as powerful forces of nature and can be invoked to aid in your work.

❖ The Greek Pantheon - includes gods and goddesses such as Zeus, Hera, Apollo, and Athena, and are often associated with specific aspects of life, such as love, wisdom, and war.

❖ The Norse Pantheon - includes gods and goddesses such as Odin, Thor, and Freya, and are associated with strength, power, and magic.

❖ The Hindu Pantheon - includes gods and goddesses such as Shiva, Kali, and Ganesha, and are associated with creation, destruction, and wisdom.

It is important to note that these are just a few examples of the many spirit guides and deities that exist within the world of witchcraft, and you may choose to work with as few or as many as you like. You may also want to call upon a specific one for a particular reason I your work.

D. Finding You Spirit Guides or Deities

One of the most exciting parts of exploring the world of witchcraft is the opportunity to connect with spirit guides and deities who can offer a helping hand on your journey. These spiritual beings are often associated with specific elements, energies, or aspects of life and can provide insight and wisdom on a variety of topics. To find your spirit guides or deities, you'll need to start by exploring your own beliefs and values, as well as what draws you to certain energies or aspects of life.

❖ One of the most common ways to connect with them is through meditation or visualisation.
❖ Start by finding a quiet, peaceful space where you can focus and allow your mind to quiet.
❖ Close your eyes and breathe deeply, imagining yourself surrounded by a warm, comforting energy.
❖ Visualise yourself reaching out to the spirit guides or deities who you feel drawn to, asking for their presence and guidance.
❖ Repeat this exercise regularly to build a stronger connection and receive more guidance from your spirit guides or deities.

Another way to connect is through ritual or ceremony. You can create a simple ritual to honour the spirit guides or deities you feel drawn to, such as lighting a candle, burning incense, or making an offering of flowers or food. Repeat this ritual regularly to show your commitment and deepen your connection.

You can also seek out the assistance of spirit guides and deities by keeping a dream journal or being open to seeing signs and omens in your daily life. Pay attention to your dreams and the messages that come through and take note of any unusual occurrences or synchronicities that may point you towards your guide.

Ultimately, the most important aspect of connecting is your intention and dedication. The more effort you put into your practice, the more you will receive in return. So, keep an open mind, be patient, and trust in the journey. Your spirit guides and deities are waiting to offer their council to help you grow and evolve as a young witch.

A. Nature and Witchcraft

Nature and witchcraft are intimately connected, as witches often draw upon the energy and elements of the natural world in their practice. Here's an overview of the connection between nature and witchcraft:

❖ The Elements: Witches often work with the elements to create balance and harmony in their lives and the world around them. They might use elements created by nature, such as herbs, crystals, or candles, to enhance their spells and channel the elemental energies.

❖ Nature Spirits: Many witches believe in the existence of nature spirits, such as faeries, elves, and devas, who inhabit the natural world and can be called upon to assist with spells and rituals.

❖ Earth-based Traditions: Some traditions of witchcraft, such as Wicca and Druidry, are earth-based and place a strong emphasis on the connection between humans and nature.

In these traditions, witches often perform rituals in the outdoors and honour the cycles of the seasons and the moon.

❖ Connecting with the Natural World: To deepen their connection with nature and increase the effectiveness of their spells, many witches spend time in outside, meditate, and perform spells and rituals there.

By connecting with mother nature and drawing upon her energy, witches can tap into a deep source of power and create a significant positive change in the world around you. Whether through spells, rituals, or simply spending time there, the connection between nature and witchcraft is an integral part of the practice.

B. Herbalism and Witchcraft

Herbalism is a key component of witchcraft and involves the use of plants and herbs for both practical and magical purposes. Here's an introduction to herbalism and its role in witchcraft:

Herbs and plants contain unique energies and properties that make them ideal for use in spells, and other magical practices. Witches often work with herbs to enhance the power of their spells, heal physical and emotional ailments, and connect with the natural world.

Herbs can be used in a variety of ways in the craft, from making teas and infusions, to burning incense, to creating magical oils and salves. By incorporating herbs into their rituals, witches can tap into their unique energies and properties to bring about change.

Each herb has its own set of correspondences, such as its astrological sign, elemental association, and spiritual properties. By learning about the properties of different herbs, witches can choose the right ones for their work for the greater purpose.

Many witches grow their own herbs, either in a garden or in pots. This allows them to cultivate a personal connection with the plants and ensures that they are using fresh, organic herbs in their spells and rituals.

Herbalism is a rich and varied component of witchcraft that offers a wide range of possibilities for magical work. Whether you're just starting out or you're an experienced witch, adding herbs into your work can increase the power of your magic.

C. Using Plants and Herbs in Craft

Incorporating plants and herbs into spells and rituals is a great way to enhance the power of your magic and deepen your connection with the natural world. Here are some techniques for using herbs in your spells and rituals:

- ❖ One of the simplest ways to incorporate herbs into your magic is to make herbal teas or infusions. This involves steeping dried or fresh herbs in hot water to extract their energies and properties. Many stores offer pre-made tea bags filled with a combination of these herbs and spices should you not wish to create your own.
- ❖ Burning herbal incense is another way to incorporate herbs into your spells and rituals. You can create your own incense blends by mixing dried herbs and resins or purchase pre-made blends.
- ❖ Creating herbal oils and salves is a more involved process, but it can be a powerful way to incorporate herbs into your magic. These can be used for anointing candles, creating protective talismans, or massaging into the skin.

❖ You can also incorporate herbs into your spells and rituals by creating herbal charms and talismans. This might involve carrying dried herbs in a pouch, tying herbs into a charm bag, or using herbal oils to anoint talismans.

❖ Infusing candles with herbs is another way to incorporate herbs into your spells and rituals. This can be done by adding dried herbs to the wax, or by anointing the candles with herbal oils.

These are just a few of the many ways you can choose to use herbs and plants into your spiritual practice. Whether you use one of these techniques or develop your own, incorporating them into your magic can help you tap into the unique energies and properties.

D. Sustainable and Ethical Practices

Sustainable and ethical herbalism practices are important for maintaining a positive and harmonious relationship with the natural world, as well as for ensuring that the herbs you use in your magic are ethically and sustainably sourced. Here are some tips for sustainable and ethical herbalism practices:

- ❖ Make sure you know where your herbs come from and try to purchase them from reputable suppliers who use sustainable and ethical growing practices. Avoid buying herbs from companies that engage in clear-cutting or other harmful practices.
- ❖ One of the best ways to ensure that your herbs are sustainably and ethically sourced is to grow them yourself. This allows you to cultivate a personal connection with the plants and know exactly how they were grown.
- ❖ Wildcrafting, or harvesting plants from the wild, can be a great way to obtain herbs for your spells and rituals, but it should be done with caution. Make sure you understand the laws and regulations surrounding

wildcrafting, and never harvest more than you need or harm the plants in any way.

❖ Some herbs are threatened or endangered species, and it's important to avoid using them in your magic. Make sure you are aware of the conservation status of any herbs you use and consider using alternative option instead.

Remember that plants are living beings, and it's important to treat them with respect and gratitude. Say a prayer or offer thanks before harvesting herbs, and always leave a small offering in return.

By following these tips, you can create a positive and harmonious relationship with the natural world and ensure that your ingredients are ethically and sustainably sourced.

A. Why is Protection Important

Protection is an important aspect of witchcraft because it helps to safeguard both the practitioner and the people and places around them. Here are some reasons why protection is important in witchcraft:

When performing spells or rituals, it's important to be mindful of the energy you are working with. Protection spells help to direct and focus the energy in a positive and constructive manner, preventing any negative or harmful energies from affecting you or those around you.

Witchcraft can be a powerful tool for personal transformation, but it can also bring up unconscious emotions and thoughts that need to be addressed. Protection spells can help to create a safe and supportive environment for this work, guarding against any negative thoughts or emotions that might arise.

Protection spells can also help to guard against physical harm or danger. This might include protection against accidents, illness, or other forms of physical harm, as well as protection against negativity and ill will from others.

In addition to physical and emotional protection, protection spells can also help to guard against negative spiritual influences, such as spirits, entities, or energies that might interfere with your practice or well-being.

By incorporating protection into your practice, you can ensure that you are safe when practicing, and the intent remains positive, and effective. This can help to increase your confidence and ability to work with magic and create a supportive environment for your personal growth and transformation.

B. Techniques for Protection

There are many different techniques for protecting yourself and your space from negativity and harm in witchcraft. Some common methods include:

- ❖ Visualising a protective shield or bubble of light around yourself or your space can help to create a physical barrier against negative energies.
- ❖ Repeating positive affirmations, such as "I am safe and protected" can help to reinforce a sense of security and calm and create a positive energy around you.
- ❖ Smudging is a ritual that involves burning sage, palo santo, or other herbs to clear negative energies and purify the air.
- ❖ Certain crystals, such as black tourmaline or amethyst, are believed to have protective properties and can be placed in your environment or carried on your person to guard against negative energies.
- ❖ Incorporating symbols, such as the pentacle, into your practice can help to create a physical representation of protection and serve as a powerful talisman against negativity.

❖ Warding involves creating a physical or energetic barrier around your space, such as placing a line of salt around your property or using symbols or affirmations to create an invisible barrier.

By combining different techniques and finding what works best for you, you can create a strong sense of protection for yourself and guard against negativity and harm in your practice as well as daily life.

C. Maintaining Positive Energy

In addition to incorporating protection spells and rituals into your practice, there are several steps you can take to maintain positive energy and protect against psychic attacks:

- ❖ Self-Care: Taking care of your physical, emotional, and mental well-being is an important aspect of maintaining positive energy. This might include practices such as meditation, exercise, and journaling, as well as getting enough sleep and eating a healthy diet.

- ❖ Boundaries: Setting strong boundaries is key to protecting against psychic attacks. This includes setting limits with people in your life who might be draining your energy or sending negative thoughts or emotions your way.

- ❖ Grounding: Grounding is a technique that helps to anchor you in the present moment and connect you to the earth. This can help to reduce stress and anxiety and prevent negative energies from affecting you.

By adding these techniques into your work and your everyday life, you can create a strong sense of positive energy and protect yourself against negative influences and psychic attacks.

D. Protection Spells and Rituals

There are many different protection spells and rituals that can be used to guard and harm. Here are a few common ones:

❖ Salt Barrier: Creating a physical barrier of salt around your home or property can help to protect against negative energies and psychic attacks.

❖ Protection Amulets: Creating a protective amulet, such as a charm or talisman, can be a powerful tool for warding off negativity and psychic attacks.

❖ Banishing Spells: Banishing spells are used to remove negative energies or entities from a specific space or person. This might include casting a circle, calling upon protective energies, and reciting a spell or incantation.

❖ Protection Baths: Taking a bath with protective herbs or crystals, such as rose petals or black tourmaline, can help to clear negative energies, and promote positive energy flow.

❖ White Light Visualization: Visualizing a bright white light surrounding yourself can help to create a protective barrier against negative energies and psychic attacks.

❖ Protection Sigils: Creating a protection sigil, or symbol of protection, can be a powerful tool for warding off negativity and psychic attacks.

You can create a sense of security and reduce the impact of negative energies and psychic attacks by using these methods. It's important to remember that the most effective protection spells and rituals are those that resonate with you personally and align with what you believe.

A. Summary

The key takeaways from the book "Teen Witch: A Beginner's Guide to the Basics of Witchcraft" are:

❖ Witchcraft is a practice that involves harnessing energy to create change and manifest your desires.

❖ The elements, energy, intention, visualisation, and tools such as herbs and crystals, all play a role in witchcraft and spellcasting.

❖ To be an effective witch, it's important to understand the basics of energy, the elements, and how to connect with them through rituals and spells.

❖ Incorporating the phases of the moon, planetary energies, and the connection with nature, into your spell casting can increase its effectiveness.

❖ It's essential to prioritize protection in your practice, including self-care, setting boundaries, grounding, and using protective practices.

❖ Herbalism and the use of plants and herbs in spells and rituals are an important aspect of witchcraft.

❖ The most effective spells and rituals are those that resonate with you personally and align with your beliefs and intentions.

Using these key takeaways into your practice will enable you to develop a strong foundation in the basics of witchcraft and begin to create significant change in your life.

B. Grow Your Practice

As a beginner, it's important to remember that this is a lifelong journey of learning and growth. There is always more to learn, explore, and discover in. Here are a few tips for continuing your journey:

- ❖ Keeping a journal of your experiences and insights can help you track your growth and reflect on your progress.
- ❖ There is an abundance of books, websites, and articles about witchcraft, herbalism, and energy work. Continue to read, research, and educate yourself on these topics to deepen your understanding and knowledge.
- ❖ Joining a coven or connecting with other witches can provide a supportive community and opportunities to learn from others.
- ❖ Don't be afraid to experiment with different techniques to see what works best for you.
- ❖ Always trust your intuition and follow your own path, rather than trying to fit into someone else's mould.

By continuing to learn and grow in the practice of witchcraft, you will develop a deeper understanding of this fascinating and empowering tradition. Embrace your own personal journey and trust that you are exactly where you need to be, at every step of the way. Reach out if you need guidance, support or love, there are many around the world eager to share their experiences and happy to help. Remember we were all beginners once!

C. Further Education

To continue your education and deepen your understanding of witchcraft, here are some suggested books and resources:

Books:

"To Ride a Silver Broomstick" by Silver RavenWolf

"Witch: Unleashed. Untamed. Unapologetic." by Lisa Lister

"The Modern Witchcraft Spell Book" by Skye Alexander

"The Modern Witchcraft Grimoire" by Skye Alexander

"The Ultimate Guide to Tarot" by Liz Dean

Online resources:

The Witch's Book of Shadows: A website offering a wide range of articles, spells, and resources for witches.

Witchvox: A comprehensive directory of covens, events, and resources for the pagan and witch community.

The Hoodwitch: A blog offering a modern perspective on spirituality, wellness, and magic.

Workshops and classes:

Look for local workshops or classes on witchcraft, herbalism, and energy work in your community.

Online classes and workshops can also be a great option, offering a flexible and accessible way to continue your education.

Remember, the most important resource is within yourself. Trust your intuition and continue to explore and experiment with the techniques and practices that resonate with you. Happy learning!

Join my Facebook page!

(Astrid Ebonywood – Author)

Look me up directly on my authors page: -

https://www.facebook.com/profile.php?id=1000898 53896988

D. Final Thoughts

As you embark on your exciting journey as a young witch, know that you are not alone. The practice of witchcraft is rich with history, tradition, and a vibrant community of practitioners from all walks of life. Some of the best fiends I have are those from this community whom I never would have met without my craft.

Remember to be patient with yourself, trust your intuition, and never stop learning and growing. Your unique gifts and perspectives will bring a fresh and meaningful contribution to the craft and your unique way of doing things is the right way for you, there is no right or wrong.

Wishing you all the best on your journey as a baby witch. May you find joy, empowerment, and a deep connection to the magic of the universe. Trust in yourself and your abilities, and always remember to approach your practice with respect, kindness, and a desire to do good.

Blessed be, and may your path be filled with light and love always x

E. Key Terms

Here are some key terms related to witchcraft and their definitions:

Magic: The practice of harnessing energy and intention to bring about desired outcomes or effects. Magic can take many forms, including spellcasting, divination, and ritual.

Spellcasting: The process of creating and performing a spell, often involving the use of ritual, intention, visualization, and materials such as candles, crystals, and herbs.

Ritual: A ceremonial or symbolic act performed to mark a significant event, such as a full moon, or to achieve a specific outcome, such as protection or abundance.

Energy: A fundamental concept in witchcraft, referring to the unseen forces that exist within and around all things. Energy can be harnessed and directed through the practice of magic.

Intention: A powerful force in witchcraft, intention refers to the mental and emotional state behind an action or spell. Setting a clear intention is essential to effective spellcasting.

Visualisation: The practice of creating a vivid mental image in order to bring about a desired outcome. In witchcraft, visualisation is often used in spellcasting to help manifest the desired result.

Elements: The five traditional elements in witchcraft are earth, air, fire, water, and spirit. Each element is associated with different properties and energies and is often incorporated into spells and rituals.

Herbalism: The practice of using plants and herbs for medicinal, culinary, and magical purposes. In witchcraft, herbs are often incorporated into spells and rituals to enhance their power and effectiveness.

Moon phases: The changing phases of the moon have a significant impact on magic and spellcasting. The phases of the moon include new moon, waxing crescent, first quarter, waxing gibbous, full moon, waning gibbous, third quarter, and waning crescent.

Planetary energies: The movements and positions of the planets can have a powerful influence on magic and spellcasting. Each planet is associated with different energies and properties and is often incorporated into spells and rituals.

Protection: A fundamental aspect of witchcraft, protection refers to techniques and practices used to guard against negativity, harm, and psychic attack. Protection spells and rituals are an essential part of any witch's practice.

About The Author

Astrid Ebonywood is an avid student and practitioner of the craft and has been honing her skills for many years. She has a deep passion for helping others connect with their inner magic and harness the power of spirituality and witchcraft to improve their lives.

Having developed her gifts early, Astrid devotes her time and energy to enhancing the lives of others through her teachings.

And after many years of research, experience and a gaining a vast amount of knowledge, Astrid has now fulfilled a lifelong dream of becoming a writer. Allowing her teachings to branch out across the world, promoting her message of positivity, hope and love to all.

Astrid resides in the UK with her devoted Husband and has been blessed with her beautiful children.

If You Enjoyed
This Book

Please consider leaving a review on Amazon!

As a self-employed, self-publishing creative, reviews are essential to get my content out for more people to enjoy.

Your review can make a huge difference!

Thank you for being here until the end, and keep your eyes peeled for my …

NEW BOOKS COMING SOON!

Join my Facebook Page to stay connected:-

Search 'Astrid Ebonywood – Author'

https://www.facebook.com/profile.php?id=1000898 53896988

Printed in Great Britain
by Amazon

23825589R00040